THIS BOOK BELONGS TO

BORN IN ....../....../..........

———

THIS PLANNER IS NOT A LEGAL DOCUMENT AND DOES NOT REPLACE A VALID WILL.

I'M DEAD NOW WHAT?
BY TH. GUIDES PRESS

WANT FREE GOODIES?

Email us at

thguidespress@gmail.com

Title the email «DNW»
and we'll send some goodies!

Any Question?
Email us at thguidespress@gmail.com

Copyright © 2020 by TH GUIDES PRESS. All rights reserved. This book or any portion thereof may not be reproduced or used in any manner whatsoever without the express written permission of the publisher except for the use of brief quotations in a book review.

Printed in the United States of America

First Printing, 2021

ISBN: 978-1-008-99214-6

www.thguidespress.com

TABLE OF CONTENTS

My Personal Details 2

Key Contact 3

Medical Information 4

My Important Documents 5

Funeral Wishes 13

My Financial Details 19

Insurance List 23

Rental Agreement 30

Regular Payments 31

Significant Possessions 35

Useful Contacts 37

Digital Accounts 39

Access to & Location of important items 47

Arrangements For Children 49

Arrangements For Pets 53

My Personal Wishes 57

Letters For Loved Ones 67

Expression of Gratitude 81

Final Words 87

Thanks Page & Signature 95

BASIC INFORMATION

MY PERSONAL DETAILS

Full Name..

Date and place of Birth..

Social Security Number...

Address..

City........................State............................Zip........................

Marital Status ☐ Single.   ☐ Married.   ☐ Divorced.

☐ Widowed.

Father's Name...

Date Of Death...

Mother's Name..

Date Of Death...

National Insurance Number..

National Health Number...

Tax Reference Number...

Passport Number..

Driving Licence Number...

I am an organ donor   ☐ Yes   ☐ No

• Specifications : ....

....

KEY CONTACT

Full Name……………………………………………………………………

Relationship…………………………………………………………………

Phone Number………………………………………………………………

Address………………………………………………………………………

………………………………………………………………………………

Email Address………………………………………………………………

Other Information……………………………………………………………

………………………………………………………………………………

………………………………………………………………………………

………………………………………………………………………………

………………………………………………………………………………

………………………………………………………………………………

………………………………………………………………………………

………………………………………………………………………………

………………………………………………………………………………

………………………………………………………………………………

MEDICAL INFORMATION

Blood Type..

Medical Insurance Provider...

Medical Insurance Number...

Hospital......................................Contact................................

Clinic..Contact................................

Doctor..Contact................................

My illnesses..

....

....

....

....

....

Other Information...

....

....

....

....

MY IMPORTANT DOCUMENTS

MY IMPORTANT DOCUMENTS

You can use this section to note down what important documents you have, such as a will, funeral plan documents, and where they are kept. This will help your family find them when they need to.

WILL

I have made a will, and it is kept..

....

My most recent will is dated...

I have written a letter of wishes and it is kept..

....

My executors are:

Full Name..

Address..

Phone Number...

Email Address..

Full Name..

Address..

Phone Number...

Email Address..

MY IMPORTANT DOCUMENTS

FUNERAL PLAN

I have a funeral plan with……………………………………………………………

My funeral plan documents are kept……………………………………………

……………………………………………………………………………………………

POWER OF ATTORNEY

I have a power of attorney ☐ YES ☐ NO

It is dated………………………………………………………………………………

It is registered ?

☐ YES ☐ NO

MY ATTORNEYS ARE:

Name…………………………………………………………………………………….
Address…………………………………………………………………………………
Phone Number………………………………………………………………………

Name…………………………………………………………………………………….
Address…………………………………………………………………………………
Phone Number………………………………………………………………………

MY IMPORTANT DOCUMENTS

People to be contacted in the event of my death:

Name	Relationship	Contact details (E-mail, Phone...)

Name	Relationship	Contact details (E-mail, Phone...)

Name	Relationship	Contact details (E-mail, Phone...)

I WOULD LIKE THE FOLLOWING PEOPLE TO ACT AS PALLBEARERS

Name	Phone	E-mail

OTHER IMPORTANT DOCUMENTS AND WHERE I KEEP THEM

Document	Where I Keep Them
My birth certificate	
Marriage certificate	
Passport	
Other Documents	
1 -	
2 -	
3 -	
4 -	
5 -	
6 -	
7 -	
8 -	
9 -	
10 -	

FUNERAL WISHES

FUNERAL WISHES

Thinking about how you want your funeral to be - & what you don't want - will take away a lot of anxiety and uncertainty for your family.

Recording your desires and wishes means that they will have something to reassure them that they are only doing what you want.

Things you might want to think about

_____
_____
_____
_____
_____
_____
_____
_____
_____
_____
_____

FUNERAL WISHES

Write your funeral wishes here

FUNERAL WISHES

Write your funeral wishes here

FUNERAL WISHES

Write your funeral wishes here

FUNERAL WISHES

Write your funeral wishes here

MY FINANCIAL DETAILS

MY FINANCIAL DETAILS

You can use this section to record all the different accounts and financial products you have.

CURRENT ACCOUNTS

Bank/building society..

Name(s) in which account is held...

Bank/building society..

Name(s) in which account is held...

SAVINGS ACCOUNTS

Bank/building society..

Name(s) in which account is held...

Bank/building society..

Name(s) in which account is held...

MORTGAGE

Bank/building society..

Name(s) in which account is held...

MY FINANCIAL DETAILS

CREDIT AND STORE CARDS

Issuer name..

Card number...

Issuer name..

Card number...

PENSIONS

Company	Phone number	Reference number	Where documents are kept.

MY FINANCIAL DETAILS

OTHER FINANCIAL INFORMATION

INSURANCE LIST

INSURANCES

LIFE INSURANCE

Life Insurance Company..

Phone Number..

Where documents are kept...

ANNUITY POLICY

Provider Name..

Policy number...

Where documents are kept...

INVESTMENTS

Provider Name..

Name(s) in which account is held...

Phone Number..

SHARES

Company Name..

Where certificate is kept..

Company Name..

Where certificate is kept..

INSURANCES

CAR INSURANCE

Car insurance company	
Policy Number	
Renewal Date	
Where documents are kept	

CAR BREAKDOWN COVER

Policy Number	
Renewal Date	
Where documents are kept	

INSURANCES

HOUSE INSURANCE

Contents insurance	
Policy Number	
Renewal Date	
Where documents are kept	
Buildings insurance	
Policy Number	
Renewal Date	
Where documents are kept	

INSURANCES

OTHER INSURANCE (PET, TRAVEL, ETC...)

Provider Name	Renewal Date	Where documents are kept

LOANS/HIRE PURCHASE

Loan Provider	Phone Number	Where documents are kept

BENEFITS/ENTITLEMENTS

Name of benefit	
Name of benefit	
Name of benefit	
Name of benefit	
Name of benefit	
Name of benefit	
Name of benefit	
Name of benefit	
Name of benefit	
Name of benefit	

RENTAL AGREEMENT

Landlord's Name..

Landlord's Contact Details...

UTILITY PROVIDERS

My Gas Provider is...

My Electricity Provider...

My Water Company is..

My Broadband Provider is..

My Phone Company is..

My Mobile Phone Company is...

My Television Provider is...

My Local Council (for council tax) is..

REGULAR PAYMENTS

REGULAR PAYMENTS

	Name	Contacts (Email, Phone)	Payment Type
Charity Donations			

REGULAR PAYMENTS

	Name	Contacts (Email, Phone)	Payment Type
Club Memberships			
Subscriptions			

REGULAR PAYMENTS

	Name	Contacts (Email, Phone)	Payment Type
Other			

SIGNIFICANT POSSESSIONS

SIGNIFICANT POSSESSIONS

PROPERTY

Address..

....

VEHICLES

Registration number..

OTHER SIGNIFICANT POSSESSIONS/VALUABLES

Description..

Value..

Where kept..

Description..

Value..

Where kept..

Description..

Value..

Where kept..

USEFUL CONTACTS

USEFUL CONTACTS

Name	Phone number	Email
Solicitor		
countant		
Financial Adviser		
Optician		
Dentist		
Doctor		
Organisations / societies		
Neighbours (with keys)		
Other		

DIGITAL ACCOUNTS

DIGITAL ACCOUNTS

Digital possessions – from photos, videos and files stored online to social media accounts – can be just as significant as your other assets. But how will your family know what you've got? Having a record will remove the conjecture for them.

Your list might include any of the following:

• Social media accounts (for example, Facebook, Twitter...)

• Email accounts

• Online financial accounts

• Online file storage

• Online websites accounts (For example, eBay, Gumtree)

• Digital records – videos, photos and other files

• E-books

• Blogs and websites you own

• Digital currency

SOCIAL MEDIA ACCOUNTS

Social media account	Username	Password
Facebook		
Twitter		
Instagram		
Linkedin		
Pinterest		
Gmail		
Other Social Media Accounts		

ONLINE ACCOUNTS

Website	Username	Password

EMAIL ACCOUNTS

Email	Password

ONLINE FILE STORAGE
(FILES - VIDEOS - PHOTOS...)

Link	Password

BLOGS AND WEBSITES YOU OWN

Website	Password & Access information

OTHER PASSWORDS

Website	Username	Password

LOCATION OF IMPORTANT ITEMS

LOCATION OF IMPORTANT ITEMS

Access to home (keys/alarm code)..

Access to safe..

Car keys..

Important documents...

....

....

....

Password For Computer...

Password For Tablet..

Password For Phone..

Safety Deposit Box...

....

....

Firearm Details...

....

Location of Firearm Licenses...

....

....

....

ARRANGEMENTS
FOR CHILDREN

ARRANGEMENTS FOR CHILDREN

If you have minors kids, it is imperative that you choose among your family or friends who will raise them and take care of them if you are no longer alive.

The best way to do this is to write a will, and specify the assets that should be used to meet the daily needs of your minor children and if they should inherit these assets when they reach a certain age.

NOTES

_____
_____
_____
_____
_____
_____
_____
_____
_____

NOTES

NOTES

ARRANGEMENTS
FOR PETS

ARRANGEMENTS FOR PETS

If you have pets, use the space below to make a note of what arrangements you'd like to be made for them.

NOTES

_____
_____
_____
_____
_____
_____
_____
_____
_____
_____
_____
_____

NOTES

NOTES

MY PERSONAL WISHES

MY PERSONAL WISHES

MY PERSONAL WISHES

MY PERSONAL WISHES

MY PERSONAL WISHES

MY PERSONAL WISHES

MY PERSONAL WISHES

MY PERSONAL WISHES

MY PERSONAL WISHES

MY PERSONAL WISHES

LETTERS FOR LOVED ONES

Dear ....,

Dear ....,

Dear ....,

Dear ....,

_____
_____
_____
_____
_____
_____
_____
_____
_____
_____
_____
_____
_____

_____

Dear ....,

_____

_____

_____

_____

_____

_____

_____

_____

_____

_____

_____

_____

_____

Dear ....,

_____

_____

_____

_____

_____

_____

_____

_____

_____

_____

_____

_____

_____

Dear ....,

Dear ....,

_____

_____

_____

_____

_____

_____

_____

_____

_____

_____

_____

_____

_____

Dear ....,

Dear ....,

_____

_____

_____

_____

_____

_____

_____

_____

_____

_____

_____

_____

Dear ....,

Dear ....,

_____
_____
_____
_____
_____
_____
_____
_____
_____
_____
_____
_____
_____
_____

Dear ....,

EXPRESSION OF GRATITUDE

EXPRESSION OF GRATITUDE

I'm Grateful for _____

EXPRESSION OF GRATITUDE

EXPRESSION OF GRATITUDE

I'm Grateful for _____

EXPRESSION OF GRATITUDE

EXPRESSION OF GRATITUDE

I'm Grateful for

LAST WORDS

LAST WORDS

LAST WORDS

LAST WORDS

LAST WORDS

LAST WORDS

LAST WORDS

LAST WORDS

Date: ...../..../........

 # THANKS

Sorry For Your Loss - It's Me

I present my sincere thanks and my best wishes to all the special people in my life whom I have been able to trust and provide this information. I hope your continued journey to this earth will be filled with success, prosperity and love.

Name: **Signature:**

BY TH. GUIDES PRESS

<u>**LEAVE AN HONEST REVIEW ON AMAZON**</u>

WWW.BOOKART.STORE

CPSIA information can be obtained
at www.ICGtesting.com
Printed in the USA
LVHW060501220222
711685LV00007B/256